21ST Century Skills Library

COOL CAREERS
NURSE

Kevin Cunningham

Cherry Lake Publishing
Ann Arbor, Michigan

Published in the United States of America by Cherry Lake Publishing
Ann Arbor, Michigan
www.cherrylakepublishing.com

Content Adviser: Kim Amer, PhD, RN, Associate Professor, School of Nursing, DePaul University

Photo Credits: Cover and pages 1, 11, and 20, ©iStockphoto.com/jsmith; pages 4 and 24, ©iStockphoto.com/sjlocke; page 7, ©iStockphoto.com/track5; page 8, ©Pictorial Press Ltd/Alamy; pages 12 and 15, ©Andrew Gentry, used under license from Shutterstock, Inc.; page 16, ©Daniel Dillon/Alamy; page 18, ©Laurence Gough, used under license from Shutterstock, Inc.; page 27, ©iStockphoto.com/JSABBOTT

Library of Congress Cataloging-in-Publication Data
Cunningham, Kevin, 1966–
Nurse / by Kevin Cunningham.
    p. cm.—(Cool careers)
Includes bibliographical references.
ISBN-13: 978-1-60279-299-9
ISBN-10: 1-60279-299-2
1. Nurses—Juvenile literature. 2. Nursing—Vocational guidance—Juvenile literature. I. Title. II. Series.
RT61.5.C86 2009
610.73—dc22   2008006522

Cherry Lake Publishing would like to acknowledge the work of
The Partnership for 21st Century Skills.
Please visit www.21stcenturyskills.org for more information.

TABLE OF CONTENTS

CHAPTER ONE

NURSES IN HISTORY

Nurses know how to keep injured children calm.

Johnny tore off after his brother. Jeff had stolen his favorite race car for the last time. Johnny had almost caught him when Jeff dashed out the front door. The storm door whipped back. Johnny put out his arm to stop it. His arm went straight through the glass! His father took one look at the cut and knew Johnny had to go to the hospital emergency room.

A half hour later, they were led into a small room with a table, some odd-looking machines, a sink, and cupboards. Johnny was scared and wouldn't look at his arm.

A nurse came in and smiled. "I'm Emily," she said. "I hear you went through a door."

Johnny nodded.

"Okay. I promise I'll let you know everything we're going to do before it happens. I need to look at the wound." Emily peeled back the bandage that Johnny's father had put on and had a look. "Not too bad," she said.

Over the next 15 minutes, Emily took his blood pressure and brought out a giant magnifying glass to study the wound. She told Johnny and his father that there were pieces of glass in the cut but nothing too serious. Emily put a large bandage that looked like a wet napkin on Johnny's arm. It contained medicine to help ease the pain.

"The area around the cut will go numb in a minute," she told Johnny. "Once that happens, we'll use tweezers to get the glass out. Then the doctor will be in to stitch you up and you'll be set."

"Will it hurt?" Johnny asked.

"It'll sting a little bit, but the medicine will help," Emily said, and she winked at him. "We'll have you fixed up in no time."

The nursing profession we know today took shape in the mid-1800s. For several centuries before that time, nurses in hospitals were Catholic nuns or other women who had devoted their lives to religious work. Their patients were mainly the poor, elderly, homeless, and starving. These women took care of patients but

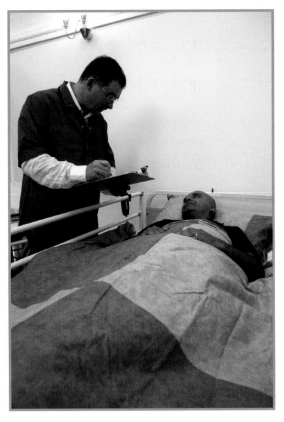

Most of the first nurses were women. Today, women and men choose to make nursing their career.

didn't have the training and education of today's nurses. Their main jobs were keeping patients warm and fed, comforting them, praying with them, and cleaning up.

By the 1800s, many European hospitals were awful places. They were overcrowded and filthy. Patients with highly contagious diseases were not isolated from other patients. It wasn't uncommon to get sick with a second illness or to have a wound become infected while in the hospital. Medicines and surgery were rarely helpful—and sometimes were harmful. Nurses of the time did not

Florence Nightingale was born in 1820.

receive medical educations. Some were known to steal from patients, ignore them, and refuse to treat them unless bribed. Sick people went to hospitals as a last resort.

Fortunately, a British woman named Florence Nightingale had some new ideas. Nightingale made her mark in 1854, when Great Britain went to war with Russia. She led a team of nurses to Turkey to nurse injured soldiers. When they arrived at a rat-infested hospital, she and her staff went to work cleaning the building. She believed that the patients would feel better if their environment were clean and well ventilated. Over the next few months, she made sure the soldiers got decent food and clean sheets and clothes. Nightingale kept track of the changes in the soldiers' health. Deaths at the hospital fell to a fraction of the number before her arrival.

She returned to Britain a hero and wrote *Notes on Nursing*. The book demanded that nurses be carefully trained in the techniques she had developed. Soon Nightingale's system was used in new nursing schools around the world. *Notes on Nursing* describes many of the things still taught in nursing schools today.

Professional nursing got another boost in 1864, when Jean-Henri Dunant, a Swiss banker, founded the International Red Cross. The organization brought professional nursing training to many new countries.

Life & Career Skills

Lillian Wald, who became a nurse in 1891, saw the needs of the communities around her and responded. She started a home nursing service to bring care into poor and sometimes dangerous immigrant neighborhoods in New York City. In 1913, her organization's 91 nurses made 200,000 visits to patients' homes. Similar groups, inspired by Wald, soon sprang up in other cities. This was the birth of public health nursing.

In 1938, nursing took another step toward becoming a profession. That year, the state of New York required that nurses earn a license to **practice**.

Over the following decades, new medicines, treatments, and types of surgery became available. Once, people simply hoped to get better. Now patients expected to get better. Nurses shifted their focus from providing comfort and basic care to playing an active part in the treatment of patients.

CHAPTER TWO

AT WORK

It is important for nurses to cooperate and work together as a team.

Nurses work in many different places. Some nurses treat patients at schools, camps, or in patients' homes. Most, however, work in hospitals.

Hospital nurses work in shifts. A common shift lasts 8 or 12 hours. A nurse starting a shift talks to the nurses from the previous shift. This lets the new shift know what's going on with the patients.

A nurse checks a patient's blood pressure.

Then the nurse checks on each of the patients under his or her care. This is called making rounds. The visit starts with taking a patient's **vital signs**. The nurse also asks if the patient has pain or discomfort. Either can be a sign of a serious problem.

If there are no problems, the nurse tends to basic care. Depending on the patient and time of day, the nurse may give medicine, check wounds, or prepare the patient for a bath or meal. Other tasks include getting a patient up and walking or talking to a patient about healthy living.

Different nurses have different kinds of duties. A geriatric nurse treats the elderly. Geriatric nurses have different tasks and issues from those that pediatric nurses encounter. Pediatric nurses treat children. All nurses, however, have the same basic goals. They want to see how their patients are doing, solve any immediate problems, and help patients get better. They also want to teach patients how to stay healthy.

Nurses rely on the patient's record, called the chart, to learn what's going on and find out the doctor's orders. Creating a patient care plan always includes **collaborating** with the doctor.

Nurses document everything they do by typing information into a computer. Keeping an accurate chart is important. It helps to ensure a patient gets consistent care from one shift to the next. It can take a lot of time. On a busy day, nurses often miss a meal or eat a few bites while typing notes. If the paperwork is unfinished at the end of their shift, the nurses must stay until it is done.

All nursing specialties are demanding. Two are considered especially stressful.

Intensive care (IC) nurses work with severely injured and sick patients. Each IC nurse is responsible for just a few patients. IC patients have a nurse with them around the clock, so the nurse on duty knows the patients well and knows what to do to keep them stable. Because IC patients are in life-or-death situations, nurses cannot always wait for a physician before acting. When an emergency occurs, IC nurses think fast and make important decisions. Hospitals provide detailed instructions, called **protocols**,

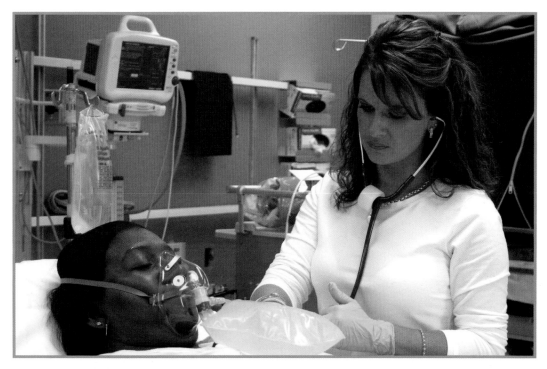

Intensive care nurses must be able to work well under pressure.

for dealing with a range of situations. But it's the IC nurses who judge what's going on and provide the treatment.

Emergency room (ER) nurses also have very stressful jobs. One minute the ER is calm, the next it's frantic. ER nurses are always ready to deal with whatever comes through the door. It might be someone with the flu. Or

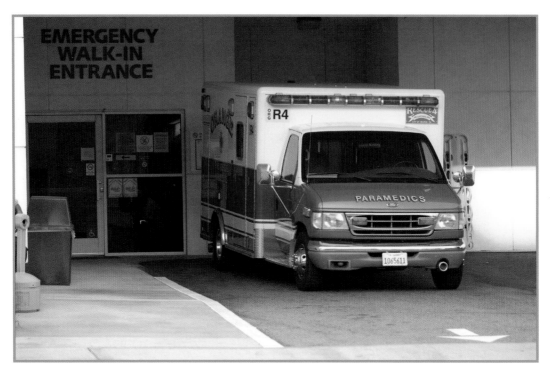

ER nurses must be able to react quickly to emergencies.

it could be several car crash victims, a man suffering a heart attack, or a woman having a baby—or all of them at once. ER nurses spend a lot of time with patients and their family members. These people are often frightened or confused by what's happened. In some cases, ER nurses talk to police officers, technicians, and paramedics to gather patient information. Once the ER staff stabilizes a patient, an ER nurse works with professionals in other parts of the hospital. This is necessary to make sure the person keeps getting the proper care.

Throughout the day, nurses constantly make decisions and cope with important responsibilities. Nursing is not a job that just anyone can handle. Success takes dedication and training along with a desire to help people. Seeing patients recover from illnesses and injuries and helping them stay healthy are just two of the profession's many rewards.

21st Century Content

Many places throughout the world do not have enough health care workers. Sometimes the shortage results from natural disaster or war. Some places lack the money or equipment to train people to provide care. Sometimes residents have little information about how to protect themselves from illness and injury. Resulting health problems are common and tend to keep occurring. Organizations such as the International Red Cross or Red Crescent, Peace Corps, and Doctors Without Borders help. They send nurses and other health professionals, as well as medical supplies, to areas with people in need. Through these and other groups, nurses are active in making sure people around the world stay healthy

WHAT IT TAKES

Taking science classes can help you decide if you want to become a nurse.

Nurse must like working with people. Future nurses also must be good at science. Biology, the study of life, is the cornerstone in a nursing career. Students begin studying biology as early as middle school. Classes in chemistry and physics provide a good background. Classes in health, **anatomy**, and **physiology** are also necessary for a career in nursing. Studying these subjects begins in high school.

In addition to studying these sciences, nurses must communicate effectively. In health care, orders must be given clearly and followed exactly. Otherwise, a patient might receive the wrong dosage of medicine or receive a treatment that could be harmful. For these reasons, future nurses need good written and oral communications skills. These skill can be improved in English and speech classes.

High school is only the first step, however. There are several routes to becoming a nurse, but all of them require continued schooling. Some nursing students begin studying at a two-year community college. There students study the sciences as well as English and mathematics. Additionally, community colleges provide students with hands-on (clinical) experience at local hospitals.

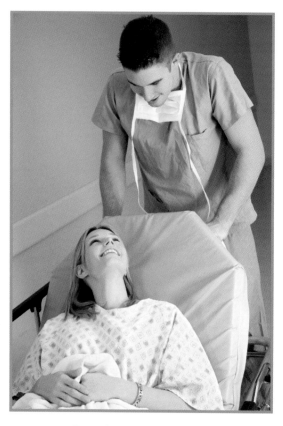

Clinical experience offers nursing students the chance to interact with patients.

Teachers and hospital staff demonstrate techniques and answer questions.

Today, it is more common for nursing students to earn a four- or five-year degree called a bachelor's degree. Nursing school, like schools for other health care professions, have become more difficult to get into because so many people apply. Good grades and volunteer experience can increase an applicant's chances of being accepted.

In the United States, Canada, and many other places, required classes include anatomy and psychology. Nursing students also take courses in nutrition, **microbiology**, physics, chemistry, statistics, and English. The early years are focused in the classroom, and the second two years on clinical experience.

After college, graduates must pass licensing tests. The tests are specific to the education and training the graduate has received.

For many nurses, the next step is to become a registered nurse (RN). That means passing an RN licensing test. Each state and the District of Columbia require these tests, though they vary from state to state.

Registered nurses and other nurses can continue their education. Higher degrees

Many nurses are members of nursing associations and organizations. Some of these groups are specific to areas of specialization, such as the Society of Pediatric Nurses. Others are for nurses in a specific location, such as the American Nurses Association. These groups hold conferences and publish journals about the profession. These resources allow nurses to learn from each other's experiences and share ideas and research about treating patients.

open up more opportunities to work as a manager, administrator, or professor and to earn higher salaries. Many professionals working on advanced degrees go to school part-time while they continue to work.

Additional training allows a nurse to specialize in certain kinds of care. A neonatal nurse, for example, cares for newborns. Newborns have specific physical and mental needs. Studying the special needs of newborns will qualify a nurse to work in a neonatal unit of a hospital.

CHAPTER FOUR

NEW TECHNOLOGY, NEW OPPORTUNITIES

Computers are great tools for organizing data. They help nurses quickly find patient information.

Nursing is the largest field in the health care industry.
Approximately 2.3 million people work as registered
nurses. Tens of thousands more work as nurse assistants

and in other nursing positions. Experts agree the numbers will grow in coming years.

It's certain that nurses of the future will have many duties different from those working today. Many of the changes will result from new **technology**.

Technology is advancing medicine faster than ever. Chemists discover new drugs. Engineers invent mechanical body parts as replacements for broken joints. Surgeons learn how to repair or replace organs in new ways.

A nurse must stay current with these advancements. Computer skills have become increasingly important. Nurses need them to access information on drugs, **nutrition**, and other aspects of a patient's care. Why? Because nurses are the medical professionals who show patients how to take a new medicine or change a bandage.

Today, about 59 percent of nurses work in hospitals. Some experts believe that in the future, more nursing jobs will be in **outpatient** care. For the past 20 years or so, the health care system has been moving away from providing medical care in places such as hospitals.

School nurses and community health nurses work within a community to help keep people healthy. They give immunizations, do blood pressure screenings, and educate people about how to stay healthy.

Today, clinics provide many of the services that hospitals used to. Health care professionals at clinics now take X-rays, draw blood, and examine a person for heart problems. Many surgeries are done at outpatient clinics.

Learning & Innovation Skills

Often, a nurse cares for a diverse group of people. Her patients can be of various ages, ethnic backgrounds, religions, and abilities. A good nurse is open and responsive to each individual's needs. How would caring for someone who is elderly be different from taking care of a young child? How might someone's ethnic background or religion affect how he interacts with a nurse?

The patient has an operation and then goes home rather than staying the night.

Nurses play a vital part in this system. Nurses often answer patient questions and give advise about minor postsurgical problems. They may also act as the link between the patient and doctor if the problems are serious.

As outpatient care increases, nurses will handle more responsibilities. To succeed, they will need quick decision-making skills, the ability to manage other people, and the willingness to learn as much as possible about their patients. Outpatient clinics will provide opportunities for people interested in working for themselves. Nurses increasingly have been setting up their own practices to provide certain kinds of care once given by hospitals or physicians.

Nursing will continue to become more specialized. Innovations in science and health are constantly increasing

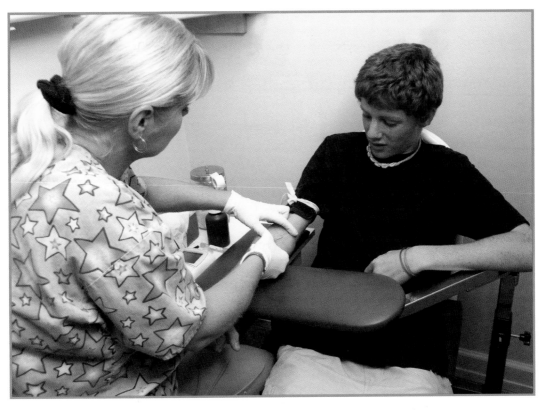

A nurse gets ready to draw blood from a patient in a clinic.

our knowledge about how to prevent and treat illness. There's a vast amount of information to learn, even within a single specialty. As medicine continues to advance, it will become harder for a nurse to move from one area to another without a big investment in time and education.

Finally, special skills can go beyond medical training. For instance, knowing more than one language qualifies as a skill. That's especially true in the United States, where most people speak only one language. Immigrants to America want, and need, care from nurses able to understand them. Nurses with Spanish skills should especially benefit, since the number of Spanish-speaking Americans is expected to grow.

SOME FAMOUS NURSES

Louisa May Alcott (1832–1888) worked as a nurse in a Union army hospital in Washington, D.C., during the Civil War. She became famous for her novel *Little Women*.

Clarissa "Clara" Barton (1821–1912) served as a Civil War nurse. In 1881, she became the first president of the American chapter of the International Red Cross.

Andrée de Jongh (1916–2007) lived in Brussels, Belgium, and nursed British airmen during World War II. As the Germans took over Western Europe, she and her father set up a secret system of houses to smuggle rescued British fliers out of the country.

Lillian Kinkella Keil (1916–2005) served as a flight nurse in the U.S. Air Force in World War II and the Korean War. She retired as the most decorated woman in the history of the U.S. armed forces.

Elizabeth Kenny (1886–1952) developed a technique for treating polio—a disease that can cause permanent disability by damaging muscles—while working in her native Australia. She later traveled to the United States to share the technique with health care workers there.

Florence Nightingale (1820–1910) first gained fame for treating wounded soldiers during Britain's war with Russia in the 1850s. Her ideas helped develop nursing into the profession we know today.

Mary Seacole (1805–1881) was a half-Scottish, half-Jamaican nurse who paid her own way to Russia to help British soldiers fighting there.

Walt Whitman (1819–1892) had published *Leaves of Grass*, a collection of poetry for which he is well known, before becoming a Civil War nurse in Washington, D.C., in 1862.

Glossary

anatomy (uh-NAT-uh-me) the study of the structures of living things

collaborating (kuh-LAH-buh-ray-ting) working together

microbiology (my-kro-by-AH-luh-jee) the study of life-forms too small to be seen with the naked eye

outpatient (OUT-pay-shuhnt) in relation to a person who visits a hospital or clinic for care but does not stay overnight

physiology (fih-zee-AH-luh-jee) the study of how living things function

practice (PRAK-tuhss) to work in one of the professional medical occupations, for instance as a nurse or physician

protocols (PRO-tuh-kolz) detailed lists of actions to take in case of specific events or emergencies

technology (tek-NAHL-uh-jee) the knowledge and tools used in a particular field

vital signs (VY-tuhl SINEZ) signs of life; a person's heart rate, breathing rate, body temperature, and blood pressure

FOR MORE INFORMATION

Books

Brill, Marlene Targ. *Nurses*. Minneapolis: Lerner Publications, 2005.

Favor, Lesli J. *Women Doctors and Nurses of the Civil War*. New York: Rosen Publishing Group, 2004.

Hinman, Bonnie. *Florence Nightingale and the Advancement of Nursing*. Hockessin, DE: Mitchell Lane Publishers, 2005.

Web Sites

KidsHealth: What Happens in the Emergency Room?
www.kidshealth.org/kid/feel_better/places/er.html
Find out more about what nurses and other workers do in the emergency room

Kids into Nursing
www.unmc.edu/nursing/careers/activities_frame.htm
For links to nursing facts, puzzles, and other activities about nursing careers

Nurse.com
www.nurse.com/students/careersinnursing.html
Information on many different nursing specialties

INDEX

ABOUT THE AUTHOR

Kevin Cunningham is the author of 30 books, including a series on diseases in history and a number of books in Cherry Lake's Global Products series. He lives near Chicago, Illinois.